Everything Left Unsaid

For It May Not Be Your Answer, But a Start

Ishaan Nandwani

INDIA • SINGAPORE • MALAYSIA

Copyright © Ishaan Nandwani 2025
All Rights Reserved.

This book has been published with all efforts taken to make the material error-free after the consent of the author. However, the author and the publisher do not assume and hereby disclaim any liability to any party for any loss, damage, or disruption caused by errors or omissions, whether such errors or omissions result from negligence, accident, or any other cause.

While every effort has been made to avoid any mistake or omission, this publication is being sold on the condition and understanding that neither the author nor the publishers or printers would be liable in any manner to any person by reason of any mistake or omission in this publication or for any action taken or omitted to be taken or advice rendered or accepted on the basis of this work. For any defect in printing or binding the publishers will be liable only to replace the defective copy by another copy of this work then available.

Contents

Dedication

"The things we create are never just our own—they carry the echoes of those who have stood beside us, believed in us, and made the journey worthwhile."

– Ishaan Nandwani

To the friend who nudged me toward writing—thank you for opening a door I didn't know I needed. A special mention to my mom and dad, for your quiet strength, steady belief, and for letting me grow at my own pace. To my brother and sister, for always being there in the ways that count. To my partner, for walking beside me and holding space for the person I've become. To my best friend, for being a constant through the years—we've grown through it all, and that matters. And to everyone who's been part of my life—whether in passing or for seasons—know that no moment was ever wasted. Each one found its place in this journey, and for that, I'm thankful.

Preface

You. Yes, you. The one flipping through these pages, deciding if this book is worth your time.

Let me tell you something—you've been here before. In the quiet moments when you question why you do the things you do. When you catch yourself repeating old patterns. When you wonder if you're changing or just circling back to the same place in a different way.

This book isn't here to give you answers. It's here to hold up a mirror—to the choices you make, the stories you tell yourself, and the truths you don't always say out loud. It's about the false starts, the near misses, the habits that hold us back, and the realizations that set us free.

So, if you've ever felt like you're running toward something but not sure what, or if you've ever looked at your own life and thought, *Wait... how did I get here?*—then this book is for you.

Go on. Keep reading. You might just find yourself in these pages.

Have you ever looked into a mirror and seen a stranger staring back?

—◆—

Not just a face you don't recognize, but a presence—one that feels both familiar and foreign, as if your past and future are trapped in a reflection you can't quite understand. For the longest time, I kept searching. Who am I? Not by name, not by role, but in the silent spaces in between. I wanted an answer—something undeniable. Something that made sense of everything. But maybe the real question isn't who am I? Maybe it's—Can I finally see myself for who I've always been? And if I can… Am I enough?

∞

Chapter 1

Privilege

It's strange, isn't it?
How some things feel like a given—until they're not.

Holding hands in public.
Kissing someone goodbye in front of strangers.
Renting or even buying an apartment together.

I never thought of it as a luxury.

Should I have? No one told me it was only for a few.

Growing up, I watched movies where people fell in love,
Effortlessly. Openly.
No whispered warnings, no second glances, no hesitation.

I never imagined love could have conditions.
I never imagined it wasn't for everyone.

Things are different now, or so they say.
But even now, I struggle to picture how it used to be.
How I used to be.

　　　

At sixteen, maybe twenty, I had questions.
Not about what I wanted to be—
But about who I was allowed to be.

Teenagers are often called a mess.
But have you ever wondered why?

Maybe because they sense something is wrong.
Maybe because they aren't allowed to feel it.

Me?
I felt it.
All of it.

I had questions, ones that could start wars if spoken out
loud.
But no one was ready to listen.

So, I stayed silent.
Because sometimes, silence is survival.

No one told me the rules,
But I learned them anyway.

What to say,
When to look away,
When to pretend something wasn't there.

Because some privileges are not taken away from you—
You simply never had them.

It started small—
The way people paused before answering.
The way they corrected themselves mid-sentence.

Like love had rules I wasn't taught.
Like the world was split in two,
And I was standing on the wrong side.

No one told me outright.
They didn't need to.
Some lessons are taught in silence.

Some things didn't need to be said.
I learned them by watching,
By noticing what was missing.

No hand-holding at family gatherings.
No invitations that included 'plus one.'
No childhood crushes spoken out loud.

Every unspoken rule whispered the same thing:
This isn't for you.

You don't unsee it, once you know.
You can't feel it less, once it's settled in your bones.

Privilege isn't just about what you have.
It is being intentionally forgetful about what you fear.

And fear?
It changes the way you move,
The way you speak,
The way you dream.

I carried it everywhere.
Like an extra shadow—
The one only I could see.

But what if I refused?
What if I took up space, anyway?
What if I reached for the things
I was told it was not mine to have?

What if I loved,
Not in the shade,
But in the open, where I am seen?

Maybe privilege is real.
But maybe, so is defiance.

&⸝⸜

Chapter 2

Unease

Was I being watched?

Did my parents notice the storm in my head?

What did being different even mean?

Why did I drift out of conversations with my friends?

Why wasn't I drawn to the girls they couldn't stop talking about?

The questions arrived before the answers.

Long before I was ready for them.

The quiet questions.

Why did I stay silent, nodding instead of speaking?
Was I just shy—or was there something else?

Maybe I had heard it too many times,
Class after class, day after day.

What was expected,
What was normal,
What was right.

But I never complained.

I nodded my way out of situation,
Avoided the games they played,
Skipped the conversations that felt like a script—
On repeat, again and again.

It was exhausting.
Yet, the more I felt, the more I questioned.

I was just a teenager, wasn't I?
And teenagers are dumb, you'd say.

I noticed the way they spoke,
The way they laughed,
The way they seemed so sure.

Sure of themselves.
Sure of the way things worked.

And me?
I was sure of only one thing—
That I wasn't like them.

They weren't cruel.
Not exactly.

But words carry weight, even when spoken lightly.
Even when disguised as a joke.

"That's weird, bro."
"That's not how it's supposed to be."
"You don't think like that, right?"

I laughed when they laughed.
Nodded when they nodded.
Pretended it was nothing.

Still, somewhere beneath the confusion,
A quiet resistance was forming.

I didn't have all the answers,
But I was learning how to guard myself.

To measure my words.
To control my expression.
To be careful.

Because I wasn't sure what would happen
If I wasn't.

It wasn't just about the words anymore.
It was about the way they made me feel—
Like I was already losing a game
I didn't sign up to play.

I wasn't just different.
I was aware of it.

And that changed everything.

The first realisation.

೩.೪

Chapter 3

Façade

Call it a double life—
Two selves, two stories.
One kept me hidden in a deep closet,
The other? Just an act.

One was convenient.
The other, unbearable.
Yet I played both roles well,
As if I had nothing to lose.

Or maybe, I had everything to lose.
And that's why I kept pretending.

Convenient for whom?
Not me.

If anything, it drained me.
Keeping up the act,
Performing the script,
Filling the silence with well-rehearsed lines.

I smiled when they smiled,
Laughed when they laughed,
Nodded when expected—
A puppet, learning its strings.

They called it fitting in.
I called it survival.

I sat in conversations,
Not because I wanted to—
But because leaving would raise suspicion.

They spoke,
And I let their words fill the room.
I forced a chuckle at their jokes,
Nodded at their opinions,
Played along just enough
To blend into the wallpaper.

That was the goal, wasn't it?
To disappear into the familiar?

Think of waking up,
Knowing you're needed.
You'd love that feeling—
At least in that state of mind.

An illusion? Maybe.
But illusions bring their own kind of comfort.
A quiet, troublesome peace.

What is comfort, really,
If it comes at the cost of self?

I let them see what they wanted to see.
They let me exist,
As long as I wasn't real.

How long could I live like this?
How long before the weight of the act
Became heavier than the cost of truth?

I looked in the mirror,
Saw a face I recognized—
But did I know him?

Two selves, two stories.
I had spent years mastering the script.
But maybe, just maybe,
It was time to forget my lines.

   EVERYTHING LEFT UNSAID

They told me I was good at this—
Blending in, making it easy.
They never asked if it was easy for me.

I laughed on cue,
Spoke when I was supposed to,
Wore the right mask
At the right time.

If I played the part well enough,
Would I start believing it too?

A mask is a strange thing—
It protects you,
But it also traps you.

I could not tell
Where the mask ended
And I began.

Was there *still **me*** beneath it all?
Or had I become the illusion
I once only pretended to be?

Chapter 4

Refrain

A constant loop of thoughts—
Should I try again?
Dim myself just a little more?
Compromise a little further?

Maybe this time would be different.
Maybe this time, I'd make a better impression.

Maybe this time, they'd stay.

I was always adjusting,
A half-step behind,
Measuring my words,
Studying their reactions.

Trying to find the invisible line—
The one between being accepted
And being too much.

Trapped in the cycle,
Drawn back to the same doubts,
Making choices not for myself,
But for the approval of those around me.

I laughed when they laughed.
I agreed when I wanted to disagree.

It wasn't lying.
Not really.
But it wasn't the truth, either.

Maybe then they'd understand.
Maybe then I'd belong.

I never asked for much.
Just a space to exist—
Without hesitation.

But I was learning,
Even the smallest things
Came at a cost.

I know now—I shouldn't have cared.
But back then, I needed to.

I needed friends.
I still don't know why.

Not that it ever helped.

I wonder now,
Did they ever need me?
Or was I just a reflection
They barely noticed?

Storms usually bring chaos.
Mine left something behind—
A silence even louder.

Not the kind that feels peaceful.
The kind that makes you second-guess yourself.
The kind that fills the gaps between people.

And in that silence,
I became smaller.
Less certain.
More afraid.

Pretending isn't harmless.
It starts as something small,
A habit, a reflex.

Until one day,
You forget where the act ends
And where you begin.

And that's the scariest part of all.

୫ஓ

Chapter 5

Disquiet

Like the jitters of newness,
The nuances of discovery—
I remained undiscovered.

Years spent in the same hallways,
Around the same people,
Yet no one ever got me.

I was still new, even after all that time.
Invisible. Shrinking.
A portrait—still, silent, unnoticed.

And the bottled-up version of me whispered:
"It is what it is."
If nothing could change, why should I?

I made peace with the walls around me.
With the quiet.
With the absence of questions.

Then it became someone else's turn.
A misdirected version of me,
Layered with haunting subtexts
No one could hear.

They assumed things.
They filled in my blanks with their own stories.
Some closer to the truth, some not.

And I let them.
Because correcting them meant revealing myself.

The chaos never lifted,
But somehow, I felt comfortable inside it.

Like standing in the eye of the storm—
Everything loud, yet eerily still.
And maybe I needed that stillness.

To feel like I belonged somewhere,
Even if it was inside my own confusion.

The questions I once had
Faded with the person I used to be.

For a second, I felt lighter.
For a minute, I felt hopeful.
For days, I was new.

New in a way that didn't need answers.
New in a way that didn't need explanations.

And I loved it.
This bottled-up version—maybe this was what I was
missing.

I felt stronger. Confident. Conversational.
Willing to take on things
I never thought I'd understand.

I laughed louder.
I spoke first instead of last.
And for once, I wasn't watching myself from the outside.

It took over. I let it.
And I couldn't stop.

At first, it was exhilarating.
Then, it was necessary.
Like armor—light to wear at first,
Then heavier with time.

But I never befriended him.

Because our stories never matched.
Our willingness never aligned.

He wanted to stay in the crowd.
I wanted to disappear into the background.

He enjoyed the stage.
I was terrified of the spotlight.

And yet, we lived inside the same body.

The tension grew louder.
Who was I pretending to be?
Who was I losing in the process?

One part of me craved the silence again.
The other thrived in the noise.

And that's when the real chaos began.

I couldn't be both.
Not forever.

Something had to give.
Something had to break.

And deep down,
I knew it would be me.

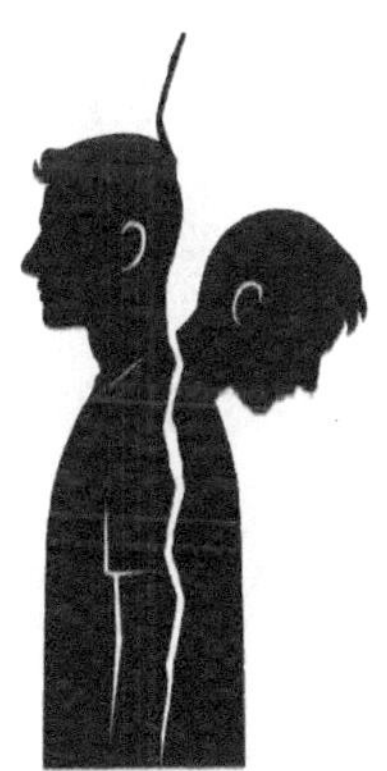

The unraveling doesn't happen all at once.
It starts with the small things.

A hesitation before answering.
A second thought before laughing.
A quiet retreat when no one is looking.

Like a thread pulled too tight,
Waiting for the first snap.

I knew I couldn't keep this up forever.
But I wasn't ready to let go, either.

Not yet.

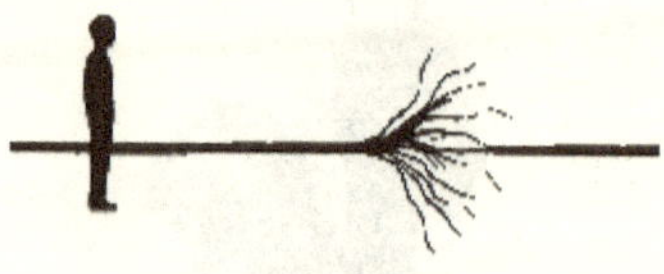

Chapter 6

The False Ally

While juggling the chaos,
A version of me emerged—
One who could overrule.
The master of disorder,
Seamlessly shifting with every curtain rise.
And yet, he despised me.

The words I never spoke
Still belonged to me.
But I had no control.
The words spoken, the choices made—
None were mine.

The harder I tried to escape,
The closer I found myself to him.
The version that stole my identity.

We were alike, and yet,
That made us even more different.
The growing rage.
The eagerness to be liked.
Maybe that's just how a teenager feels.

Or maybe—he was never meant to be my ally.

He was bold where I was hesitant.
Loud where I was quiet.
Charismatic in ways that felt foreign to me.
He could blend in.
While I stood out, even in my silence.

I let him take over.
Because he was the answer to every question I feared.
Because he knew what to say when I didn't.
Because he understood how to survive in places where I
never belonged.

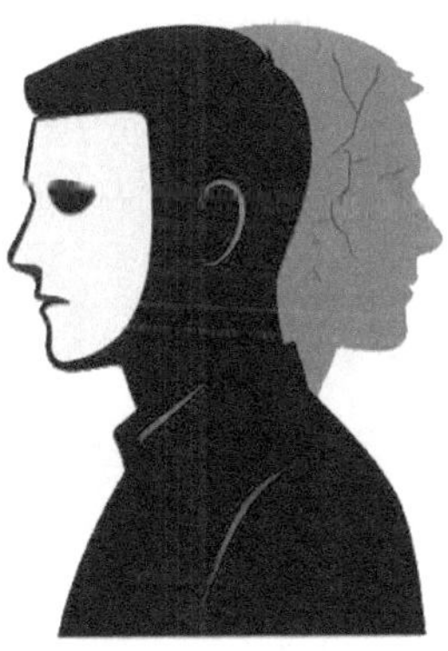

But he wasn't me.
He couldn't be.
And yet, the world welcomed him.
They laughed at his jokes.
Shook his hand.
Called him one of their own.

So I let him stay.
Because if I didn't—who would I be?

Then the cracks begin to show.
A hesitation in his voice.
A slip in his mask.
The illusion fading, even if no one else noticed.
But I noticed.

He wasn't invincible.
He was just pretending.
And once I saw it, I couldn't unsee it.

I wanted to rip him apart.
To reclaim what was mine.
But how do you fight something you created?
Something that, despite everything, kept you safe?

Did I even want to let him go?
Would I disappear without him?
Or worse—would anyone care?

Some lies keep you alive.
Some illusions keep you moving.
But at what cost?

He was never meant to stay.
But I had held onto him for so long,
That I wasn't sure where he ended
And I began.

What happens when the mask you wear
No longer fits?
When the false ally becomes the enemy?

I was about to find out.

∞

Chapter 7

Resurgence

While I searched for his weakness,
I looked closer for mine.
If he was as smart as I feared,
He must have been doing the same.
And I was right.

Just as I planned my next move,
He had already made his.
He had always been one step ahead,
A shadow I couldn't outrun.
But then—something shifted.

My fight was never with the world.
It was with the narcissistic, idealized version of me.
The one I built to survive.
The one I thought I needed.
But he was never real.

I wanted him to lose.
Not because I hated him,
But because I couldn't afford to be him anymore.
I never realized how much my identity mattered
Until I almost lost it.
Why did I let it get this far?

It was time to stop holding back.
Even as haunting questions
Made me judge myself over and over,
I learned to face them instead of running.

For years,

I convinced myself

That he was my armor.

That he protected me from a world

That demanded too much.

But he was just a disguise.

A crumbling mask I could no longer wear.

This wasn't a battle of fists.

I wasn't going to punch myself into submission.

No loud declarations.

No dramatic endings.

Just a quiet realization—

He was only strong as long as I let him be.

Even acknowledging my old self
Made him weaker.
And then—he crumbled.
And I?
I broke free.

Freedom felt unfamiliar at first.
Like walking into a world
That had always been there,
Yet never within reach.
I hesitated.
Not out of fear,
But because I had forgotten what it meant to move without restraints.

A deep breath.
A step forward.
And suddenly,
I wasn't looking over my shoulder anymore.
The past didn't disappear.
But it no longer defined me.

I had won.
But winning wasn't an ending.
It was the beginning.
There was no roadmap for what came next,
No instructions on how to be whole again.

But for the first time,
That uncertainty didn't scare me.
I wasn't searching for another version of myself.
I was learning to exist as I was—
Unfiltered. Unburdened. Unafraid.

And maybe that was the real victory all along.

☙

Chapter 8

Reckoning

Often found in books,
For once, I saw it in the mirror.

A transformation—quite literally.

Once I learned acceptance,
I thought I'd never turn back.

It was time for my next chapter,
The one I locked in a mental closet.
I wanted to give it a shot,
Let it linger—
Just to see where it would lead me.

Realistically?

I was curious.

What would a new constant feel like?
Could I handle the 'all eyes on me part?'

Could I answer the question: What now?

It consumed a part of me, and I let it.
Mistakes happened, and I let them.
The why me syndrome circled around me—
And I let it.
For the first time, I was in control.

I thought acceptance was the end of the journey.
Turns out, it was just the beginning.

Now, I was ready to speak.

ॐ

Chapter 9

Reconciliation

Long ago,
I made a promise to my younger self—
One day, we'd sit, talk,
Share secrets only we could understand.

It was time.
I had enough to offer him now.

And so, we met.

The café I loved—he didn't mind it either.
The coffee I ordered—he asked for the same.
Blueberry cheesecake—
I introduced him to it, and boy, he adored it.
It was about time.

We slipped into conversation effortlessly.
Not unexpected, yet I had thought it would be.
Now don't ask me why.
Imagine meeting your younger self—
Wouldn't you hesitate, too?

As we talked, curiosity sparked in his eyes.
A mind unburdened,
Untouched by knowing,
Unaware that knowing wouldn't change a thing.

Out of nowhere, he asked—
"Does it get better?"

The words hit me like a nail on a plank.
The silence carried a quiet resonance,
Awaiting the weight of my answer.

The choice was mine.
Should I tell him plainly?
Or let him figure it out as life unfolds?

I could shield him with false hope.
I could risk him hating me for the truth.

With hesitation, I said nothing but honesty—
"It gets tougher from here on.
But that doesn't mean you won't handle it. Trust me."

Maybe all he needed was reassurance.

We talked and talked,
As if we had been waiting for this moment forever.
And though I was having the best time,
I held back—
Because too much would take away his free will.

I wanted to warn him.
I wanted to tell him how one wrong decision
Could shift everything.
But I let him carry his own burdens,
As I had carried mine.

We shared memories,
Wove stories into something we thought would last.
But nothing does.
No warnings. No second chances.

And now, the moment had come—
Not to lose, but to let go.
Not to forget, but to finally make peace.

We stood up.
One last glance.
A quiet understanding.

And then, we left.

෴

Chapter 10

Liberation

Autumn—
A season of release,
Of shedding what no longer belongs.

The clingy past.
The echoes of yesterday.
The worn-out confusions.
The weary charisma.

It was time.
And I let go.
(You should too.)

Healing.
A word so versatile,
A state so complex,
A journey so simple.

I took the liberty to embrace it—
Not because I was entitled to,
But because I chose to.
I was confident.

Life took its turns.
People took theirs.
I accepted.

Hard at first.
Simpler as it went.

Some called it cowardice.
Others, negligence.
I accepted both.

I laughed and said, "Maybe."
I laughed again, but this time—
I said nothing.
I walked away.

Pause.
Let the moment sink in—completely.
Do not let go just yet.
It's too soon.

Even if it hurts, trust me—
It's too soon.

Struggle for answers.
You may find some.
Sometimes none.

Ask yourself—
"What would I have done differently?"
"Can I do anything now?"

If yes—do it.
If no—let it go.
Believe that it has run its course.

It was hard for me at first.
It isn't anymore.

&

Chapter 11

Reclamation

Freedom wasn't in breaking chains.

It was in knowing they were never mine to carry.
I let go—
Of silence. Of hesitation. Of the weight of not doing
anything.

I decided. I will speak my part.
Whatever comes next—I can handle it.

And so, I did.

I set my story free. Once too difficult to express—

Now, I let it breathe.

I came out to my family. They paused, but listened—
overjoyed.

We talked. We celebrated. It was renewal.

I wish I could have told Dad, But breathing in the peace—
Bet he knew!

Dad... His absence was a presence in itself. A silence that filled the room, wrapping itself around me in moments I least expected. I closed my eyes and saw him—hands folded, eyes carrying the kind of wisdom that needed no words.

Maybe you've felt this too—the weight of a conversation that never happened. The ache of love never spoken aloud. Would they have understood? Would they have accepted you for all that you are?

I longed for his voice. But time had already taken him somewhere I couldn't follow. Still, when I spoke my truth, I felt him—not in sorrow, but in the quiet certainty that his love had never been conditional.

Mom... You are everything living—wind, fire, earth, breath. The constant force that steadied me. It's because of you that I am here. That I stayed. Where his silence taught me to listen, your presence taught me to feel. I never had to explain myself. You already knew.

Between the two of you, I learned this:

Love doesn't always need words.

It shows up—in silence, in strength, in staying.

But freedom comes in waves. Even after the first breath of
relief,

Doubt lingers.

A voice asks—

Will they see me differently now? Will love remain
unchanged?

I reminded myself: Love that changes was never real to
begin with.

And theirs—

Had always been real.

My story was never just mine. I just didn't know.
I reclaimed my peace. And that was healing.
It could have gone sideways. But it didn't.
That's what happens when you let go.
It was MY story to tell; Became OURS to live.

For years, the burden felt endless.
And in one moment—I forgot.
Then, I remembered. Not as a pain, but a proof.
I cherished. I cried. I was unburdened. I reclaimed peace.

And for the first time in years,
The past didn't pull me back.
It stood beside me.
A part of me—but not all of me.
This was mine to own. And I did.
A sky without weight. A moment unchained.
The beginning of something new.

෨෧

Chapter 12

Belonging

They say love isn't meant to be caged.
It isn't something you find—it finds you.
It isn't something you own, yet it becomes a part of you.
It cannot be measured, yet it shapes you.

My younger self wouldn't have understood this.
Love felt distant to him—
Something for others, never for him.

But I have walked this path now.
And one day, he will too.

Healing is often painted as something soft, gentle.
But in truth, it is raw and unrelenting.
It doesn't just soothe you; it breaks you first.
Takes everything you thought you knew,
strips it bare,
and asks—Are you ready to feel everything?

And I did.

The sadness. The joy. The jealousy. The rage.
I let it all in.

I thought healing was the end of the journey.
But it was just the beginning.
Because with healing came acceptance.
And with acceptance came something I never expected—
A kind of freedom I had never known.

And then, there was him.

He didn't know he was missing love.
Not in the way I had.
Not in the way that keeps you up at night,
wondering if you'll ever find it.

But love doesn't always arrive with a grand entrance.
Sometimes, it's just there.
In the quiet moments, in the spaces between words.
In the way you don't have to explain yourself—
because, somehow, they already know.

We weren't looking for love.
We weren't waiting for it.
But it found us anyway.

Because healing doesn't just make you whole.
It makes you open.

Open to joy.
Open to pain.
Open to love.

And when you are open,
love has a way of walking in—
unnoticed at first,
until suddenly, it's everything.

This wasn't about finding another person.
It was about finding myself in the presence of another.

And in that presence, I didn't shrink.
I didn't pretend.
I didn't perform.

For the first time—
I just was.

And that was enough.

☙❧

Chapter 13

Beyond the Mirror

But first, let me thank you.
For coming this far.
For reading, for imagining with me.
For taking it all in.

This chapter belongs to you.
To the seekers, the ones who dared to look beyond the surface.
The ones with the soul of a star.

Every day, you learn.
Every day, you express.
Every day, you reach beyond yourself.

And if no one has told you this yet—
You have already achieved.
Not by comparison.
Not by measuring up.
But by looking back.

To who you were a year ago.

Five years ago.

To the version of you who once whispered, *You won't make it.*

And yet—

Here you are.

Breathe.
You did good.

Look back. Look beyond the mirror.
Did you find it?

Proudly—I did.
And I'm glad I did.

附ﬄ

...Finally

The reflection no longer asked me who I was.
No longer challenged me, mocked me,
Demanded an answer I couldn't give.

Because, finally, I knew.

For so long, I had searched for validation from the echoes of
my past.
Waiting for something—or someone—
to tell me I was enough.

But the truth had always been simpler than I made it.

It wasn't about fixing the past,
Or rewriting the chapters I wished had gone differently.
It was about accepting—
That every version of me had mattered,
Had built me,
Had led me here.

So, I stepped away from the mirror—
Not as a question,
But as an answer.

For the first time,
I no longer searched for closure.
I no longer asked, *Why?*

I allowed life to remain open-ended.
Not as an unfinished story—
But as an unfolding one.

And that was enough.

%

Is It The End?

In the end, the mirror did not break.
It did not shatter under the weight of my past.
It simply stood—
Holding every version of me,
Every reflection that once felt incomplete.

And at last, I saw it.

A reflection that did not ask to be explained.
A reflection that did not need permission to exist.
A reflection that had always belonged.

I stepped forward.
I smiled.
And I walked away—whole.

No more echoes, no more doubt.
Just footsteps leading forward—
And the quiet certainty
That I was always enough.

৪১৯

 EVERYTHING LEFT UNSAID